THE
WEALTHY
TRADIE

RETIRE RICH, RETIRE YOUNG
AND HAVE FUN ALONG THE WAY

Hugh Bowman

"WEALTH IS NOT JUST MONEY; IT'S ABOUT TIME, RELATIONSHIPS, FAMILY, AND HEALTH."

- HUGH BOWMAN

The Wealthy Tradie. - 1st edition
ISBN: 9 780645 094312

CONTACT:
Hugh Bowman
Ph: 0409 402 474
Email: hugh@actioncoachgeelong.com.au

www.wealthytradie.com.au
www.actioncoachgeelong.com.au

CONTENTS

Introduction

Why Tradies Everywhere Are Running
Their Business Backwards!

Let's cut straight to the chase: If you're reading
this, there's a high likelihood you're running your
business backwards.

Most tradies would say their business has probably
taken over their life. You have no time to scratch
your backside, let alone check your profit and loss,
and if you were honest with yourself, you'd probably
agree that you're not running your business - your
business is running you!

You're tired. You're frustrated. You're probably not
even sure if you're making enough money for all the
effort.

Over the past 11 years, I've had the opportunity to
coach hundreds of business owners across a wide
range of industries – and over the last five years,
I've worked exclusively with tradies on how to
grow their businesses in a way that's sustainable,
profitable, and cashflow-positive.

And I've got to tell you – all tradies seem to be drowning in the same types of problems. They have no time. They've got little or no idea what their finances are doing. They know something needs to change in their business, but they have no clue how to fix it.

I get it. I really do. I've started, stopped, sold and ran many businesses since 2003, and it can be tough. Your staff is whining or simply dropping the ball. Your customers are paying late but you're too busy to follow up with them. Your "to do" list is getting longer every day, and instead of ticking off boxes, you're putting out fires or simply pushing through. It seems no matter how much blood, sweat, and tears you put in, it just doesn't stop! Everyone wants a piece of you. And then when you come home, you've got to do the bloody books.

It's exhausting, right? I mean, you knew business wouldn't be a piece of cake, but you didn't expect it to be this hard.

Well mate, here's the thing...

You're running your business backwards!

In fact, almost all business owners are, even if they're NOT drowning and are actually doing a lot of things "right".

See, most tradie owners are way too caught up in the day-to-day running of their business.
They're stuck on the tools, they're running around like a headless chook doing the quoting, or they're busy chasing up suppliers or customers.

Have you ever stopped to ask yourself, " "Why the heck am I doing this?"Wait, don't answer that. Of course you have. Every business owner has (on more than a few occasions) wanted to pack the whole thing in and go work for someone else... and then gritted their teeth and got on with the job.

The better question to ask is, "What is my ultimate and personal reason for doing this?"

A lot of coaches out there will tell you it's to grow their company. You might even believe that's what you need to do too. Sure, go ahead! Let's just grow the damn thing. And seeing as it's already in a pickle, let's double our problems while we're there!

The Accidental Owner

Most tradie business owners are what I call accidental owners. A lot of time they just ended up as the owner of their own business. They figured they could do a way better job than their boss, so they went out and started working for themselves. Or they were great on the tools and figured becoming the owner was the next logical step. Maybe their boss simply handed them the keys and said, "Mate, you run it." (This happens more often than you think – can you now see why?)

Most tradie owners don't come with a Master's Degree in Business or previous experience in running a company. In a lot of cases, they didn't preplan it so they go into business with their eyes wide open on how to manage finances, time, people, systems, and suppliers… they just wing it, and have been flying by the seat of their pants ever since.

This leads to all sorts of unnecessary headaches that you yourself are probably experiencing right now. But like I said, you're absolutely not alone when it comes to running your business backwards, because it's not just tradies who struggle with this, it's almost all business owners out there, myself included before I discovered the better way.

(This came through experiencing great difficulty first, which I don't recommend.) And it's THE answer instead of just flying blind by spending more on marketing or hiring a new team member or throwing whatever business trick at a problem you haven't really identified.

What's Different About this Book

What follows in this book is not what some business guru in his garage has cooked up that consists of basic business principles that he'll flog off to you for a ridiculous price. What follows is the ACTUAL solution to your business problems.
What follows is a new way of looking at your business and how you build REAL wealth through it.

Real wealth is not only about the dollars. Obviously, the money is important, but real wealth is also about having time, energy, optimal health, and great relationships.

Do you think you are currently succeeding in each of these areas? Of course, you're not!

The reality is working around the clock leads to frustration and exhaustion... not real wealth.

Most of us aren't chasing luxury yachts, living the life of the rich and famous or building massive business empires. We just want a business that spins off a nice profit, is easy to run, and gives us back the choice as to whether we go to work or not.
Despite what you've been led to believe, you don't need to grow big to get rich. And you don't need to bust your guts to get wealthy either. What's required is this: the ability to think a little differently, measure what must be measured, and tweak a few key areas in your business so that it funds the life you want to live.

This book is different for three reasons:

1. Everything I teach you in this book is "evergreen"
    – this means the proven 4-step system I guide
    you through will work for you and your business
    today, tomorrow, and forever. Even if your
    circumstances change, the beauty of this system is
    that it will still work for you.

    We're not talking about cheap business tricks here
    – this is the one and only book you'll need to read
    if you want to build wealth through your trades
    business.

2. I don't just write and teach this stuff. I actually do this myself. I smoke what I'm selling and I swear by this system! I started using the first tool I talk about in this book over 15 years ago. This was long before I knew what I was doing or that it would be great for business.

   I was just ticking along, tracking my personal wealth and not thinking too much about it. Later (and after experiencing pain), I would connect the dots – and even then, it would take my own business coach to tell me that what I was doing was well worth sharing.

3. We don't start with your business, we start with YOU! Look, you'll find a truckload of business books out there that'll teach you how to grow your business, but what's missing is a really big deal - the owner!

   What's the point of being in business if you don't get the perks of actually being a business owner – like having more money, more freedom, more flexibility and more power? Let's face it, we don't all want the same things in life, and we don't all want (or need) the same things in our business. So we first start with you, and then get the business delivering you what you want.

This is a tailored solution to become a Wealthy Tradie who lives life and runs his business on his own terms.

The Missing Piece

The reason almost all business owners are running their business backwards is this: They're missing a key piece of the puzzle! They've been led to believe they need to put all the effort into the business without giving any thought about themselves.

Can I be frank? *Your business isn't your baby – your life is significantly more important! The missing piece is to get your business to fund your personal wealth.*

Remember: Wealth is not just money, it's the whole kit and caboodle.

If you're like almost every owner out there, you've got it the wrong way. You should never structure your life around your business. You structure and build your business around the life you want to live, and you do this by following this simple but proven system - to build wealth through your trades business. We work out what you want and then we get your business to deliver it for you.

It's simple, really. But this vital link between personal wealth and business success seems to be glossed over everywhere. And when it IS mentioned, it's just that – mentioned. There isn't a system that "reverse engineers" it for you.

You need to work backwards from what you want to achieve on a personal front (like paying off your mortgage, buying a couple of properties, taking a trip around Australia, or building a nest egg so you can retire wealthy and early without breaking your back) and then deliberately sets up action steps to take in your business to fund this dream life. Literally no one else seems to be doing this. And I've certainly never seen one that's made specifically for tradies by a guy who works with them every single day. If I'm honest with you, I wish I had created it earlier just for myself.

The 4 Step System: How This Book Works

Have you ever gone to the doctor, said nothing, and had them hand you a script of exactly what medicine to get? Of course not! They don't know what's wrong with you!

Likewise, my proven system to become a wealthy tradie follows a similar method.

It consists of four simple and highly effective steps:

1. Clarify: the doctor asks you what's going on
2. Plan: you get a script
3. Do: you take your medicine
4. Review: you go back for a check-up

What you'll learn in this book is the essential first steps:

- how to dream big
- how to set inspiring goals
- how to track your wealth and growth and...

Why it's awesome if you have a business that you can use as the engine for your wealth creation.

Get excited because you're about to get the exact system that will take you from A (what you want) to B (having it) as quickly and efficiently as possible.

It is literally life changing.

The Author's Story

How I Bridged the Gap Between Personal Wealth and Business Success.

Before I kick off the proven 4-step system to build wealth through your trades business, I want to tell you who I am and why I'm qualified to teach this. Of course, you can skip this chapter and go right into the meat and potatoes if you couldn't care either way. On the other hand, if you're wondering "Who on earth is this guy and why should I even bother reading this book?" then there's a couple of things about me you might find interesting.

How It Began

My business mindset first began when I was growing up on a sheep and cattle farm. I learnt a lot of practical skills, as well as the value of an honest day's work. In fact, my first business was related to the farm. I made a stock whip (what you use to move herds of cattle) in my year 10 leather-making class, and my dad reckoned it was good enough to sell to other farmers. Before I knew it, I had my own little stock whip business on the side! It only lasted a year or so, but it's funny how early the entrepreneurial streak shows itself.

I also remember when I was about 11 when there was a mouse plague in large areas around Victoria and our barn was infested. Instead of just throwing around a bunch of traps and hoping for the best, I came up with my own solution to the problem.

It sounds a bit gross and I suppose it's a bit of a strange story to tell given we don't know each other too well just yet, but here's what I did: I grabbed an old wine bottle, leant it over a bucket of water and put a bit of cheese on the end of it. Low and behold, a mouse would spot the cheese, run along the wine bottle and it would slip off the neck of the wine bottle into the bucket. Down goes the mouse. This would happen again and again and before I knew it – and here's the yuck part – there was a bucket of one hundred drowned mice!

Business is like this minus the sea of rodents, of course. It's about solving problems in unique ways. It's about getting the job done, but it's also about maximizing the effort you put in to get the best results from your efforts. In the case of my unpleasant mice story:

Why set and reset heaps of traps when you can make just one really good one that won't require any extra effort from you?

Where It Went

This unusual and practical thinking is probably what got me studying engineering and then later, business. My engineering career was an interesting one and it allowed me to tackle some really cool projects as well go on to run several businesses.

I worked in an industrial refrigeration business which led to a larger consulting business, and then finally working as the managing director for an engineering start-up which came with lots of surprises that a Master's Degree in Business won't ever teach you, like how to manage people, lead a rapidly growing business, and juggle a lot of spinning plates without going crazy.

Amid all this, I also studied and practiced share trading and property investing. I'd been "quietly" investing in shares since I was a teenager, but this interest had begun to take on a life of its own. It was exciting to check on my stocks every week or so and see an uptick in their value. Mind you, with the "up and down" nature of shares, some weeks were much better than others, but more often than not I was a happy camper.

Because of this new obsession, I started reading a lot of business and investment books whenever I got the chance, and it was during this time I became quite the fan of a guy named Jim Rohn. He was a very successful American entrepreneur, author and motivational speaker.

To give you an idea, he was worth more than $500 million when he passed away at age 79 so he obviously knows a thing or two about business. I read his book, 7 Strategies for Wealth & Happiness and another book by Russell Conwell called, Acres of Diamonds (which is based on the idea that there's "acres of diamonds" or wealth buried in your very own backyard). The lessons in these books profoundly shifted something in me.

At the time, I was still working as managing director for an engineering company. I'd been working crazy hours, had a young family and was living in Geelong, a town about an hour southwest of Melbourne. I was making this commute every day and wondered which part of me would break first – my business, my family or me. So, I listened to my inner voice and made the call. I was going to use the skills I'd already learnt to start my very own business!

This led me to join the franchise business company called ActionCOACH in 2011, but it wasn't all smooth sailing because while I was great at coaching, I wasn't always great at taking my own advice! At this time, I coached many different businesses ranging from industries like professional services, retail, health, consulting and trades.

I quickly got swept away in the excitement of business instead of focusing on the longevity of business. I also started, sold, part-owned and owned several businesses during this time. (I strongly discourage splitting your focus in this way unless you really know what you're doing.)

These businesses – a burger restaurant, an online grocery business, and a medical practice – all came with their own lessons (some regretful ones), and while these life learnings weren't always great for me, they did become invaluable teachings for my clients who could learn through me what NOT to do in their business!

Again, some advice: I strongly discourage learning the hardships of business directly (a lesson I obviously learnt the hard way.) The best way to avoid making mistakes in business is to learn these mistakes from someone else. I put it down as my "practical" learning to my formal business qualifications – ultimately, the university of life is the best teacher!

Gratefully, I also enjoyed business success along the way too, which boosted my ability to pass the right information on to my clients, information that's best learnt through practical and personal experience.

Why Tradies?

After working with countless small business owners, it became apparent to me that I really enjoyed working one-on-one with tradies.

I generated the best results with these types of owners and a somewhat obvious realisation kicked in: I had spent most of my life working with trades. It explained why we both "got" each other and how I was able to understand their businesses in a way many other coaches just couldn't. I knew the lingo because I lived it.

In my engineering days, I worked with several different trades to get a job done so I knew their world. I also knew their pain because I'd personally seen and experienced it myself. So, I made the pivot and decided to work exclusively with tradies in 2017, and I've hit the ground running ever since.

It's been a privilege to see my tradie owners work directly on their business, see their mindset shift to one of a business owner (instead of just an operator), and best of all, see their revenue grow on average of 50% a year!

Why I Wrote This Book (The No "B.S." Version)

The motivation to write this book came from several factors, but the largest one was a marital separation in 2019 where all my future plans – both personal and financial – derailed to such an extent, that they required a complete restart. I got divorced, I lost 75% of my assets, and felt like I had to start from scratch.

I am a father of five boys under 13, and yes, it gets busy in our household. I think we all know or can imagine that divorce can get messy, mean, and set you back many years if you're not careful.
So, after thinking it through, I decided to cop the financial hit on the chin, and get on with life.
It meant my now ex-wife could keep the house and my kids could keep some normality in their lives.

It meant handing over the keys to the big houses, medical practice, and investments my wife and I had busted our guts to create from scratch all those years. It meant walking away from the vast majority of my wealth and watching my retirement plan fly out the window at 46 without any backup plan to speak of.

It was a tough time, to say the least. But it made me rethink everything, which pushed me into necessary action. The greatest lesson you can take from pain is the necessity to change.

So, I pivoted. Quickly!

Because of my age and circumstance, I knew there was no room for error. I had to think really carefully about where I was and what I wanted – and what my kids and I both needed in life today AND tomorrow. I had to bridge the gap between where I was and where I needed to be as quickly and as safely as possible, and I had to figure out how the bloody hell to retire at a reasonable age while still being able to enjoy the lifestyle I craved in the here and now.

It seemed almost too hard, but I had no choice but to buckle down and get smart with how I worked, how I spent my money, and how I leveraged the assets I still had to my name.

What you'll read in this book is the exact system I used to restart my future. I took pretty much every lesson I'd learnt in life up until that point – in both business and in the wealth creation space – and built a simple system for myself, and it worked. In fact, I am still using it and it is still working. But most important is no one should EVER have to lose almost everything before they realise how important this system is.

Concerned, I started asking my tradie clients,

"Hey, do you have enough in Superannuation?" or
"Are you on track to paying off your mortgage?" or
"Do you invest anywhere outside the business?"

Most tradies would look at me with a blank stare! Some didn't even pay themselves Super; others didn't know how they were getting through the day, least of all how they were setting themselves up for the future; and others were as oblivious to their personal finances as they were to their business finances!
They were just not thinking of this stuff at all. I saw how hard they worked, yet at any minute, the house of cards could fall on top of them, and it would all be for nothing.

I was invited to speak to the Lara Chamber of Commerce and at a regional ActionCOACH conference about my business philosophy where I took the opportunity to talk about this new connection I'd made between personal wealth and business.
Again, I was met with heaps of wide eyes! There was a massive gap there for almost every business owner, even some of the most successful ones.

They just weren't, and still aren't, thinking about this stuff. It seems we're all so caught up in running our businesses, that we're not putting much, if any, effort into making sure our business delivers what we want and need personally.

If your business isn't even making sure your basic needs are met (both now and in the future), don't you think something vital is missing?! I personally think so, and I don't think you should wait until you lose almost everything to realize just how important this stuff is.

If I could pass on anything, it would be this: Running a business is tough. Anyone who says it's easy, is trying to sell you something. There's a reason why more than 60% of small business fail within the first three years and why less than one in ten make it to where I am, and perhaps where you are, which is past the ten-year mark.

There are a lot of moving parts involved, and if you don't understand how these parts all work together, things can fall apart pretty quickly. Either that, or as the owner who is responsible for everything, you keep copping the brunt of it - going and going until your wheels fall off. This is not the solution.

The answer (what I wish I knew before I even got into business and what I took more seriously as I continued on my own journey to wealth), is to align your business to your personal wants and needs so that it becomes a tool to enrich your life, rather than a headache you have to constantly deal with.

My hope for you is to caretake your own future and unlock the potential in your business in a way that is truly beneficial for you and your loved ones. I hope that starting from today, you go on to become a truly wealthy tradie.

STEP 1: CLARIFY

How to Get Clear on What You Want and Where You are Financially

Chapter One

Is This You?

When was the last time you sat down and got crystal clear with what you were doing in business? Last week? Ages ago? Never? And what about the last time you sat down and got crystal clear about your personal dreams and financial position? Last week? Ages ago? Err, what the heck are you talking about?

Business coaching is tricky. Of course, you would think it's all about the "how to" in building a profitable business, and it is, but here's a spoiler for you: There's no point being in business if you don't get the perks of being in business.

Case in point: Could you take the next three months off and feel assured that your business would survive perfectly without you?

If not, you haven't mastered the art of reverse-engineering your business strategy so that it purposely lines up with what you want to achieve personally. Yes, I'm talking about that 3-month road trip up north, the early retirement, or the half day / half week / hands-completely-off-the-tools arrangement, or anything you want.

Welcome to the Clarify Stage of the Wealthy Tradie System! Here, we get clear on what you want and where you sit financially. In terms of my proven system to build wealth through your trades business, this is where you currently sit:

CLARIFY

Take the Test:

Any change starts with getting clear on where you are right now. With that in mind, do any of the following behaviours or attitudes sound like you?

- I am not clear on exactly what I want in my personal life.

- I have no idea how my personal goals relate to my business goals.

- I don't know how to arrive at my business goals.

- I have no goals or plans to speak of.

- I don't regularly monitor the progress I'm making in my business.

- I don't have time to tick this stuff – I'm too bloody busy!

- I'm neck-deep in the weeds of my business.

- I am still flat out 'on the tools' in my trades business.

- I feel like I am putting out fires, not building my business.

- I find business management stressful.

- I have no clue where all the money is/goes in my business.

- I've got a team supporting me, but the job now seems harder, not easier.

- I can't find great employees.

- I have no idea how much my net worth is.

- I'm not on top of my finances (business and/or personal).

- I don't have systems set up correctly in my business.

- I struggle to market my business.

- I'm drowning with work, but I don't have much to show for it.

- I don't know how much I need to retire.

- I need help to work ON my business instead of just IN it.

- I haven't really stopped to reflect on what I'm doing with my business.

- I don't know what to do in my business to take it to the next level.

If you ticked one or more, the good news is, you're in the right place! Once you finish this book, you will breathe a sigh of relief because you will be clear on what you want and where you want to go; you will know what your net position and business value is; you will have set some concrete goals in place to focus on and have a clear roadmap to follow; and – the big one – you will know EXACTLY what you need to do next in your business to get the cashflow needed to fund the lifestyle you want!

No need to pull 12+ hour days when you learn the better way to do business. And that is just the start of it…

Ready to get your business working for you? Let's do this!

In the next section we are going to get clear on two things:

What you want and where you are now.

We will cover a lot of stuff, but the free tools I'm super excited to show you are:

- W.I.S.H List
- The Wealth Tracker
- BizValue Calculator

Chapter Two

The #1 Question Every Trade Owner Needs to Ask But Often Doesn't!?

The very first thing we want to do when working out how to build wealth through your trades business is to get really clear on one fun question:

What do you want?

As a business coach who works exclusively with tradie owners, I've found that very few people actually spend much time thinking about their ideal life or what their dreams are for the future.

I hate to break it to you mate, but here's the truth: You're not in business to flog yourself with work, have no time for the wife and kids, constantly put out fires, juggle office work and customer complaints, manage yet another headache with the suppliers, or feel like every day comes with another thing to add to your overflowing plate.

If that's your dream, good on ya. But if you're like the vast majority of us small business owners, you're probably keener on the profit and boss privileges, right?

Remember – you're the owner. This means you need to take a step back, look at the bigger picture, and figure out why the heck you're going through the effort to run a business in the first place.

At the end of the day, there are only two rules of success – one is to figure out what you want, and the other is to go and do it. So, consider this section as tackling Rule #1 on your success journey!

Right now, we're going to help you answer this question:

If you had unlimited time and money, what would you HAVE, what would you DO, and who would you BE?

The Aim of the Game

Basically, we're going to create something like a "bucket list" of all the things you'd love to do. There's no limits or timeframe on this, so you can come up with whatever dreams you have. Think 5, 10, 20+ years out. I've explained a great way to do this below, including some examples. It's like a bucket list on steroids. (And yes – it's more powerful than you might think.)

W.I.S.H List

I first had a crack at coming up with my own version of a bucket list years ago, and between you and me, I thought it was rubbish. In fact, one of the tools I have access to as an ActionCOACH is called "Dream Builder". It's a bucket list of sorts, but it asks you questions about your dreams and includes separate questions that fall under these three categories:

- What would you like to HAVE?

- What would you like to DO?

- Who would you like to BE?

Although I initially still used this tool, I was put off by some of the questions it asked. For example, it asked me, "How many helicopters and airplanes would you like to own?"

I thought this was pretty out of touch with reality and not something I was personally interested in. Still, I stuck with it but secretly felt only half-invested in it.

Fast forward a few years. I found myself with a spare ticket to see a guy named Sebastian Terry. He's a local guy here in Geelong who became a motivational speaker after overcoming a personal challenge when his dad died. Basically, he got really burned out and depressed – similar to a midlife crisis but at the age of 25. As a result, he ended up coming up with a bucket list of his own.

He called his list "100 Things" and that's exactly what it was – a list of 100 things he'd love to do before he died. It was full of hilarious and fun things like scooter across Australia, throw a dart on a map and visit the country it lands on, and meet Shane Warne. I loved how light-hearted and exciting these were.

In the process of writing my own version, I felt it didn't address the practicalities in life such as what type of house I wanted, where I wanted to send my kids to school, what I wanted my career to look like, and when I wanted to retire. I had things like a motorbike trip in New Zealand, a ski trip to

Switzerland, and an Australian road trip with
my brother.

So, here I was – I had two tools I was half-heartedly
using, but neither really scratched the itch on what
was important to me. That's when I had the ol' light
bulb moment and realized I needed BOTH!

The good news is I've come up with a tool that does
exactly that – combines both. It has the "Have, Do,
Be" element of the Dream Builder tool, but it also
has room for all the fun stuff.

I've called it a W.I.S.H List — W.I.S.H stands for
What I Should Have. Basically, it's a simple and
fun way to capture your dreams and desires! I chose
an acronym just to make it super easy for you to
remember and apply. It also gives you room to
revisit and make changes based on what phase of
life you're in because let's face it, today you might
be dreaming of that caravan trip around Australia
before the kids are teenagers, but soon enough, you
might pivot your thinking to what sort of life you
want to be living when you retire.

I ran this exercise with my clients recently and some
of the cool things they included on their list were:
cave dive in Mexico, run a marathon, create a share

portfolio, sky dive, go to Antarctica, consolidate
their business, take a road trip around Australia
following the supercross, buy the building they rent,
own their dream car, travel Europe, watch Carlton
in the Grand Final, take part in the Conondale
Classic… you get the gist.

W.I.S.H List
My "What I Should Have" List

Remember – put on your dream shoes. Nothing is
too big, ridiculous, or too much here! Throw it out
there and see what sticks. You're much more likely
to have your dreams come true when you know what
they are, right?

QUESTION: If money, time, and resources were
NOT an issue…

What things would you like to HAVE?

- HOUSE(s) – What's your ideal home? Where is
  it? What does it look like? How many bedrooms?
  How big is the shed out back? What about the
  holiday house?

- VEHICLES – Cars? Motorbikes? Caravans? How
  many and what are they?

- TOYS – If money wasn't an issue, would you own
  a boat? What about a jet ski? Bikes? Surfboards?

What things would you like to HAVE? (cont)

- ELECTRONICS – How much tech equipment would you own if you were living your dream life? (How many computers, stereos, toys, phones, tools, motorized tools, garden tools?

- PETS – You've got all the money (and cleaners) in the world. What pets would you own? Dogs, cats, birds, guard dogs, fish, etc.

- INVESTMENT PROPERTIES – How many? Residential? Commercial? Land? Farms? HOW BIG?

- SUPERANNUATION – How much?

- SHARES – Equities, managed funds, blue chips, tech/biotech, mining, retail, transport, etc.

- CASH – How many bank accounts? How much cash in each?

- BUSINESSES – Do you just have one or many? What's the turnover/profit, number of employees, number of offices/stores, industries, etc.

- JEWELLERY – If you and/or your partner could have any piece of jewellery you wanted, what would you have? (watches/necklaces/rings)

- COLLECTIBLES – art, furniture, memorabilia, jewellery

What would you like to DO?

- MAJOR ACHIEVEMENTS – What are the big wins in business? With family? Investing? Sports/hobbies?

- DONATIONS & CHARITY – How much are you giving back? Who do you support? For how long?

- KID'S MONEY – How much, when, what rules, etc.

- SPORTS AND SPECIAL EVENTS – Now that you have more time, what sport are you playing? Are you going to any gigs? Are you seeing any shows or sporting events?

- HOLIDAYS – Where? How many weeks per year?

- HOBBIES – What cool stuff are you doing just because you can?

- NATURE – Are you spending time at the beach? Camping? Up a ski mountain? Write down where you are, what you're doing in nature and how often you are there.

- HEALTH AND FITNESS – What are you doing to keep fit and healthy? Where? What? How often?

- RESTAURANTS AND SHOWS – How often are you going out for dinner? Takeaway? Special treats?

- FUN TIMES: are you running with the bulls? Skydiving? Cycling around Australia? Taking a Formula 1 race car for a spin? Traveling in Europe?)

What sort of person would you like to BE?

- FRIENDSHIPS — Now that you have heaps of money and time, who are you hanging out with? What friendships do you have?

- FAMILY — How are you showing up for your family?

- ROLES — How are you showing up in your roles? Parent? Business owner? Son? Daughter? Friend? Brother? Sister? What percentage of time are you spending in each role?

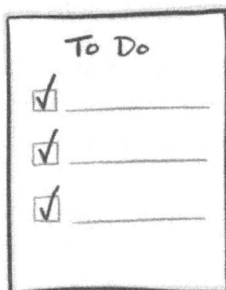

ACTION ITEM

Fill out your W.I.S.H List

Your turn to have a crack at filling out your own
"What I Should Have" (W.I.S.H) List!

If you would like a free printable PDF copy
which could be useful if you have a partner
and want to make sure you're on the same
page with each other, simply head to:

www.wealthytradie.com.au/freestuff

- Remember there is no timeframe to complete your lists of dreams and wants – think 5, 10, 20+ years out.

- The aim is to get you to think beyond this month or year.

- Think BIG: the thinking is, "Given unlimited time or money…"

- Your items can be weird things, popular activities… whatever floats your boat!

- The bigger your dreams, the more you will achieve.

- The bigger your bucket list, the more fun you will have ticking the items off.

- The clearer you are about your dreams and the more effort you put towards them, the more likely you are to achieve them.

- This might be your first crack at it, so aim to add things to it and tick things off at least once every year!

- Download the free PDF copy of the W.I.S.H list so you can simply fill in the blanks, from

www.wealthytradie.com.au/freestuff

Chapter Three

Understanding Your Wealth Position

Do you know how much you're worth?

Years ago, my own personal business coach asked me a similar question to this. Instead of just replying, I opened my laptop, double-clicked on an Excel spreadsheet I'd been working on and showed him.

He looked at my screen, stared for a bit, and then turned back to me.

"Wow, okay. So, I presume you do this with all your clients?"

That caught me off guard.

"Err, no." I replied.

"Well mate," He said, "You should. I honestly don't know any other coach who's doing this."

I suppose in some ways, that conversation is what started this whole book in the first place.

You see, on my laptop screen was something I didn't know was unusual back then. It was just something I did and had done for the last fifteen years, so it was normal to me. That's why I had no idea it was valuable, and certainly had no idea that it was something I should be sharing with my own clients!

Here's the thing: I know EXACTLY how much I am worth down to the dollar, and I know when my wealth position is going up, down, or nowhere!

But I'm getting ahead of myself.

Right now, I'll show you how to get clear on your current wealth position - how much you and your business are worth so that you're ready for your next step. And later on I'll show you the really quick tweak to turn this information into a system you can run on repeat that'll only take you 15 minutes every 6 months to complete, if that. Sound good?

What's Your Financial Position?

Now that you are clear on your dreams and the big W.I.S.H. for your life, the next step is to identify and record where you are right now, financially speaking.

This includes things like:

- How much is your mortgage?

- How much is your business worth?

- How much super do you and your partner have?

- Do you have investments, cars, etc.?

You will soon see step-by-step instructions on how to do this, but first be aware that the act of putting all this financial information in one place has many benefits. Not only will this help us to figure out your net worth, it's usually a huge eye-opener as very few people ever go to the small effort of figuring out how much they really have to their name. You might be surprised at what you find out, but it also helps us identify the gap between where you are and where you want to go which will allow us to create the plan to bridge this gap.

We will do this in Step 2.

There's also another really important reason why we want a very clear picture of your current financial position. If we know where you are now, we can review this information again and track your wealth over time.

Oh, and just so we're crystal clear on what we mean by "net worth":

ASSETS
(Things you own that have value)

–

LIABILITIES
(Money you owe)

=

NET WORTH

The Types of Assets to Measure

The type of assets we want to measure in this step are things like your home, your business, investment properties, cars, boats, motorbikes, shares, and superannuation - basically anything of big-ticket value.

A good rule of thumb here is anything you own that's worth more than $5,000-$10,000. We are also

going to work out how much your business is worth.
You will find instructions in the next chapter for that.

Please note: any vehicles that are attached to the
business do not need to be included for the purposes of
this exercise. They will fall under business value, so for
this section, just focus on your personal assets.

Don't get bogged down in the weeds. Rough values
are okay for the point of this exercise (especially if it
means you'll get it done). Just be mindful not to count
things twice.

How Do I Find Out How Much My Assets Are Worth?

For help in figuring out how much your
assets are worth, see below:

- Home and property – www.realestate.com.
au or look at recent sales
- Cars – www.carssales.com.au
- Boats – www.boatsales.com.au
- Motorbikes – www.bikesales.com.au
- Superannuation – get in touch with your
personal superfund
- Cash balances – your bank account/s
- Business value – see the next chapter for
step by step instructions.

The Types of Liabilities to Measure

Generally, this will be things like home loans, investment loans, personal loans, credit cards, etc. Again, anything that is attached to the business is not included here.

How Do I Find Out How Much My Liabilities Are?

If you don't know where to go to find out how much money you owe, see below:

- Home & investment loans – check your statements or go to your bank branch.

- Credit card – check your credit card statements.

- Personal loans – check your loan statements or go to your bank branch.

- Car loans – check with your car loan provider or go to your bank branch.

Step-by-Step Instructions

1. Write down all the assets you own, including how much they are worth.

2. Write down all the liabilities you have, including how much you owe.

3. Add all the assets together and subtract your liabilities to get your net worth. -or-

4. Skip the work and just get "The Wealth Tracker." It's a free tool that'll total it for you and let you track your wealth.

Download if from
www.wealthytradie.com.au/freestuff

WAIT!

Why Do We Want to Track Your Wealth?

When you begin to track your wealth position by looking at each asset value, you'll notice that each of these items will change quite a bit. For example, house prices go up, business values change and cars and toys go down in value.

The thinking behind it is not just to get a sense of how much you own at any given point in time and whether or not your assets are growing. It's because it is hugely rewarding and inspiring to see your net worth change over a period of time.

The psychology behind it is when you regularly check these numbers, you will be even more motivated to make positive changes in your business so that these numbers increase even more!

The tool we use to measure your wealth position is called The Wealth Tracker.

The Wealth Tracker

The Wealth Tracker – or TWT for short — is a tool that identifies all the assets you own worth more than $5,000 or $10,000 and their value at a specific point in time. For example, if you currently own a house and today it's valued at $960,000, you would list this as one of your items in your TWT with today's date.

Here's an idea of what that might look like:

	start date	
Assets		
Home	$	960,000

If you continue with this particular example and stick with today's values, you would add in all of the assets you own.

In the following table you can see that along with the home, we also have a business that's valued at $433,000, an investment property, a couple of cars (not tied to the business), a motorbike, a boat, and some cash sitting in the bank. So, we make sure all these values are listed.

		start date
Assets		
Home	$	960,000
Business Value (see last tab)	$	433,000
Investment prop 1	$	540,000
Investment prop 2	$	-
Car 1 (Non business)	$	50,000
Car 2 (Non business)	$	35,000
Motorbike	$	15,000
Boat	$	25,000
Super Partner 1	$	120,000
Super Partner 2	$	40,000
Shares	$	15,000
Bank account - Personal 1	$	23,000
Bank account - Personal 2	$	10,000

Liabilities - personal		
Credit Card(s)	$	-
Home Loan 1	-$	500,000
Investment property loan 1	-$	400,000

Once this is all done, we can step back and let the tool run the numbers. And guess what? We see that our net worth is $1,366,000!

		start date
Assets		
Home	$	960,000
Business Value (see last tab)	$	433,000
Investment prop 1	$	540,000
Investment prop 2	$	-
Car 1 (Non business)	$	50,000
Car 2 (Non business)	$	35,000
Motorbike	$	15,000
Boat	$	25,000
Super Partner 1	$	120,000
Super Partner 2	$	40,000
Shares	$	15,000
Bank account - Personal 1	$	23,000
Bank account - Personal 2	$	10,000
Liabilities - personal		
Credit Card(s)	$	-
Home Loan 1	-$	500,000
Investment property loan 1	-$	400,000
Nett Worth	$	1,366,000

The best thing about this tool is once you start tracking these values every six months (which we will do in Step 4 when we conduct our review), you can see the percentage change in your net worth.

It's amazing to see this increasing, especially if you continue to build on your asset base and get smart with how you run your business.

You will literally see your net worth increase right before your eyes! From personal experience I can tell you there's nothing quite like it.

It's very motivating to keep you focused on what most matters and on what will most move the needle on your financial position.

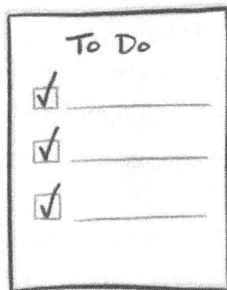

ACTION ITEM

Fill out the Wealth Tracker

Fill out The Wealth Tracker – it's completely free:

www.wealthytradie.com.au/freestuff

FYI – Don't forget to include your business value! How to work out your business value is covered in the next chapter so you can easily revisit whenever you need to.

READ ON....

QUICK
TIPS

- Don't let this exercise daunt you. The intent is to just put rough values as a starting point.

- You will get a huge eye-opener once you work out your net worth.

- It'll make you see things differently – ie., when was the last time you really thought about how valuable your super was?

- Once clear on these numbers, we can set some realistic goals to improve your overall financial position.

- The entity that owns the item doesn't really matter in most cases. We're interested in your net worth in a manner that's easy to understand and update. Again, be mindful not to include cars that are owned by the business if we're including the business value.

Chapter Four

How Much is Your Business Actually Worth?

How do you value your business?

Valuing your own trades business is always very interesting. A lot of my tradie clients usually expect their business to be worth nothing!

On the flipside, you just need to take a look at a business broker's website and see that businesses for sale actually seem very expensive… and yes, they do sell at these prices!

So clearly valuing businesses can be tricky. There are many factors at play, and ultimately it will always come down to this:

The value of your business is what someone is willing to pay for it.

That said, there is a rule of thumb to work out the value. I recommend you use this standard methodology below each time. It just makes the process easier and quicker for you:

MULTIPLE OF REPEATABLE PROFITS

+

ASSETS

–

LIABILITIES

=

BUSINESS VALUE

This oversimplified rule of thumb is multiple of repeatable profits, plus assets and less liabilities.

Let's break it down.

What's a Multiple?

A multiple is a number used to demonstrate what a business is worth. In simple terms: the higher the multiple number, the higher the value (worth) is expected to be.

It reflects the Return On Investment (ROI), and is both an art and a science to work out the correct multiple for any given business. In the real world when determining the value such as a business, a buyer has to evaluate many factors - industry risk, economic risk, staff turnover, inaccuracy of financials, behaviour of current clients, behaviour of previous owner, continuity of suppliers, and many others things.

All these factors, plus the fact that all buyers have varying levels of risk acceptance, will affect the expectations of value and the multiple used.

In general though, the multiple for small trades businesses vary from 1 to 4.5 depending on the likelihood of repeatable profits (explained further below).

The table below will help you choose the right multiple for your business:

Business description	Multiple
One- to three-man business. All knowledge in owner's head. No contracts in place.	1
Most 3- to 30-man businesses	2 – 3
Larger business. Managers in place. Long term customers with contracts. History of good and increasing earnings.	4+

Repeatable Profit

Repeatable profit is the amount of profit you can reasonably predict to receive in the future based on the previous years' profits.

While assets and liabilities in your business are fairly easy to estimate, the level of certainty of repeatable profits is the major concern for anyone buying the business. For example, five years of increasing profits would give a buyer quite a lot of confidence in future profits; whereas, if in the same five years you had three years of reasonable profits and two years of low profits, the buyer would have less confidence in the business and therefore would not offer as high a multiple of earnings.

Using the following table, I have highlighted how I might estimate a repeatable profit. Basically, you would list the amount of proft a business has had over the years to see if you could determine a trend. This is what a buyer would look for if they were looking to buy your business. They want to know how healthy it is from a profit point of view.

Now, you don't always need to go back five years to determine this like I have outlined below. For a rough business value, an understanding of your previous year's profit (or even the last two years) should be okay.

That said, it's great for a business owner to get an understanding of how this works.

EXAMPLE: Trades Business #1						
Financial Year Profit (FY)					Estimated Profit *a rough indication	Multiple (Based on the estimated profit)
2018	2019	2020	2021	2022	2023	
$160K	$210K	$180K	$130K	$320K	$200K - $300K	3

EXAMPLE: Trades Business #2						
Financial Year Profit (FY)					Estimated Profit *a rough indication	Multiple (Based on the estimated profit)
2018	2019	2020	2021	2022	2023	
$90K	$70K	$80K	$20K	$21K	$86K	1

HEADS UP!

Something Worth Noting

Something else worth noting is that if your profit does increase, the overall valuation increases by more than just the increased amount in profit because of the multiple. This would further improve your business value and is a great way to increase your overall net worth!

EXAMPLE: Business Value
Let's take a look at a sample business so that it really lands for you!

Using my BizValue Calculator tool, I've captured all the key metrics we need on an Excel spreadsheet. Here's the full picture of what this business looks like. (I'll break down all these numbers so you can see how we got to our total business value of $433,000).

The Business Value Calculator Tool

See table on the next page…

BIZValue Calculator		
Balance Sheet		
Assets		
Current		
Cash	$ 55,000	
Accounts recievable	$ 47,000	
Other	$ -	
Fixed		
Vehicle - Ranger	$ 50,000	
Vehicle - Hilux	$ 15,000	
Machinery - Excavator	$ 45,000	
Truck & Float	$ 140,000	
Equipment	$ 15,000	
Other	$ 17,000	
Total Assets	$ 384,000	
Liabilities		
Current		
Accounts payable	$ 32,000	
Taxes & GST payable	$ 35,000	
super payable	$ -	
Other		
Non-Current		
Loan ranger	$ 40,000	
Loan Truck	$ 95,000	
Loan Excavator	$ 25,000	
Total Liabilities	$ 227,000	
Nett Assets	$ 157,000	
Profit and Loss		
Profit - previous year	$ 138,000	
Net Profit	$ 138,000	
Business Value Calculation		
Nett Assets (asetts less liabilities)		$157,000
Choose Profit Muliplier (2.0 if unknown	2.0	
Profit (from above)	$ 138,000	
Multiple of profits		$276,000
Business Value		$433,000

Let's break down the numbers. This trades business has a combined total of $102,000 in current assets (cash and accounts receivable) and $282,000 in fixed assets (machinery and equipment). If we add the two together, this business has a total of $384,000 in assets.

BIZValue Calculator		
Balance Sheet		
Assets		
Current Assets		
Cash	$	55,000
Accounts recievable	$	47,000
Other	$	-
Fixed Assets		
Vehicle - Ranger	$	50,000
Vehicle - Hilux	$	15,000
Machinery - Excavator	$	45,000
Truck & Float	$	140,000
Equipment	$	15,000
Other	$	17,000
Total Assets	$	384,000

Their current liabilities include $32,000 in accounts payable and $35,000 in taxes + GST payable. They also have loans attatched to their machines and equipment worth a total of $160,000. This means they have a total of $227,000 in liabilities.

Liabilities		
Current Liabilities		
Accounts payable	$	32,000
Taxes & GST payable	$	35,000
super payable	$	-
Other		
Non-Current Liabilities		
Loan ranger	$	40,000
Loan Truck	$	95,000
Loan Excavator	$	25,000
Total Liabilities	$	227,000
Nett Assets	$	157,000

Now we subtract our total asset value from our total liabilities value to get the real story of the net assets in the business which is $157,000.

BIZValue Calculator

Balance Sheet
Assets

Current Assets

Cash	$	55,000
Accounts recievable	$	47,000
Other	$	-

Fixed Assets

Vehicle - Ranger	$	50,000
Vehicle - Hilux	$	15,000
Machinery - Excavator	$	45,000
Truck & Float	$	140,000
Equipment	$	15,000
Other	$	17,000
Total Assets	$	384,000

Liabilities

Current Liabilities

Accounts payable	$	32,000
Taxes & GST payable	$	35,000
super payable	$	-
Other		

Non-Current Liabilities

Loan ranger	$	40,000
Loan Truck	$	95,000
Loan Excavator	$	25,000
Total Liabilities	$	227,000

Nett Assets	$	157,000

If we go back to our rule of thumb on "How To Value a Business," our rule is:

MULTIPLE x REPEATABLE PROFITS
+
ASSETS – LIABILITIES (NET ASSETS)
=
BUSINESS VALUE

So in this example, we now know the net assets. Let's put it in:

"MULTIPLE" x REPEATABLE PROFITS
+
$157,000

We also know that the multiple for this is business is 2. Let's put that in:

2 x REPEATABLE PROFITS
+
$157,000

Based on our profit & loss statement from the previous year, we know that the profit we made was $138,000 as illustrated:

Profit and Loss		
Profit - previous year	$	138,000
Net Profit	$	138,000

So we'll put that in as our Repeatable Profits section:

2 x $138,000

+

$157,000

=

BUSINESS VALUE

If we plug all the numbers into our equation, we can see that our business value is **$433,000.**

Business Value Calculation			
Nett Assets (asetts less liabilities)		$	157,000
Choose Profit Muliplier (2.0 if unknown)	2.0		
Profit (from above)	$ 138,000		
Multiple of profits		$	276,000
Business Value		$	433,000

The Client Who Was Looking To Purchase a Business – How We Valued It!

As a business coach, I usually end up buying or selling a couple of businesses with clients. One such example is Stuart who owns a local electrical company here in Geelong. He was busy doing his thing when another electrical business came up for sale that had some great customers, good staff and equipment, and excitingly, because it dealt with a different area of electrical, it could help leverage his current business in a desirable direction.

Stuart got in touch with me to see what I thought about him buying the business, so our next move was to value this prospective business to see how much it was worth and what Stuart should offer for it if he went ahead with the purchase. Luckily, we had already studied and applied valuation techniques to Stuart's own business, so we reached out to the same expert accountant to run a full evaluation of this electrical business. What we found was interesting to say the least.

Sales of the previous years of this prospective business were relatively consistent, but the profit flip-flopped between $-80K and $104K with an average of -$25,000 as shown below. Before seeing this, we had obviously been hoping for consistent profit or increasing profit, so we were initially surprised and quite concerned with these numbers.

	2019	2020	2021	Average
Sales	$978K	$1,135K	$964K	$1,026K
Profit	$-80K	$104K	$-101K	$-25K

Then the accountant made several "addbacks" (these are expenses that get added back to the profits of the business) including depreciation, an apparent private vehicle put through the business, salaries and super for the associates.

The seller also claimed there was some cash taken and personal house renovations also put through the business that were skewing the profit results shown. After the accountant applied these adjustments, we could see that there were actually three profitable years.

Now, given Stuart would need to employ someone to run his current business or this new one (depending on where he allocated his time), the purchase would have to allow for the cost to employ a manager. So we added in this cost to get a more accurate relection of what the profit would look like. The manager salary was presumed to be $115,000 a year.

	2019	2020	2021	Average
Profit after addbacks	$97K	$293K	$67K	$152K
Less manager salary	$115K	$120K	$120K	$118K
Adjusted profit	-$18K	$173K	-$53K	$34K

Based on the previous table, you can see that the average profit was estimated to be $34,000. We agreed that the assesment of goodwill (the reputation of the business) as shown by the accountant allowed for low profitability and inconsistant earnings, so the profit multiple or return on investment that we used was 2.5.

The goodwill (multiple x repeat profits) was then valued at:

2.5 x $34,000 = $85,000

Assets in the business were valued at around $100,000, which meant our valuation of this business was a total of $185,000.

At the time of writing, the seller was after $500,000+ for his business so there was little point in negotiating unless the owner was willing to take a lot less.

While you might not be buying a business, this exercise highlights several very important things:

- It's crucial to know how to value your own business.

- Understand all the factors that affect business value. It's more than just a quick "rule of thumb."

- Having several years of true financials when hoping to sell your business is key.

STEP 2: PLAN

How To Create a Plan That Bridges the Gap from Where You Are to Where You Want to Be!

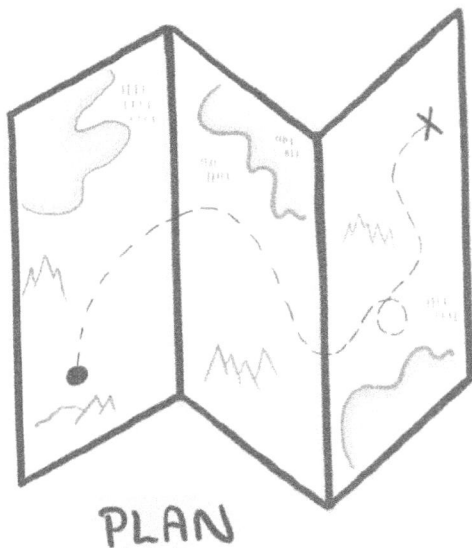

PLAN

Chapter Five

The Ultimate Blueprint to Get What You Want in Life and Business

Now that you know what you want and have an idea of where you sit financially, it's time to bridge the gap between where you currently are and where you want to be!

We do this by setting some goals, putting some financial parameters in place (yep, a good ol' budget!) and coming up with a step-by-step plan of action. This plan will serve as the blueprint for getting exactly what you want.

The reality is most tradie owners struggle to put a plan in place, or simply don't know how to create one that isn't more work, a headache, or doesn't

deliver on what they actually want and need.
So, I'm going to walk you through the specifics to make this a breeze for you.

The wise Benjamin Franklin once said, "If you fail to plan, you plan to fail," and I reckon he was onto something. If you want to turn your dreams into a reality, you must first put dates around them (turn your dreams into goals) and work out exactly what you need to do (the strategy) to achieve them.

This means you can focus your energy on the right things and quit doing the things you don't like or don't give you tangible results. Spontaneity can be a good thing, but not when it comes to your small business.

... WELCOME TO THE PLAN STAGE OF THE WEALTHY TRADIE SYSTEM!

Here we create a plan that bridges the gap from where you are to where you want to be. In terms of my proven system to build wealth through your trades business, this is where you currently sit.

In this section we are going to come up with a tailored roadmap to:

- Turn your dreams into realistic goals.

- Create a financial plan that excites you, not restricts you.

- Discover what your business needs are to make your dreams a reality.

PLAN

Chapter Six

Goal Setting 101 for Tradies

By this stage you've thought about your dreams, and you know where you are financially.

Did you notice a gap between where you are and what you want? Good. Now's the time to start thinking about turning your dreams into goals.

Goal setting is the first plan of action we set for ourselves. Not only will it keep you accountable and motivated, it'll make sure you get s#it done. So, as we move through this section of the book, start thinking about what dreams you might want to prioritize so we can turn them into goals.

Please note: we want to create PERSONAL goals before we develop business ones. We'll tackle business goals in the business section of this book. I know most tradies can list those business goals off the top of their head anyway. For now, let's focus on what YOU want first).

If you have a lot of dreams, it would be a big mistake to have an equal number of goals. Too many goals can become overwhelming very quickly. My suggestion is to start with just a few big goals and maybe a couple of smaller ones. I dive deep on how to set a budget around your "Big Ticket" items in the next chapter, but here we'll set the scene and look at the best strategy to turn your overarching goals into concrete, realistic ones. For example, you might come up with a personal goal like:

- Pay off my home loan.

- Contribute more $$ to my super.

- Go on the caravan trip around Australia.

- Buy an investment property or build a share portfolio.

- Have $ amount in savings.

- Get my weekends back!

And while these are all great as overarching goals, they don't have enough meat on the bones. This means you're less likely to stick to them. At the end of the day, a goal without a date is just a dream so you want to make sure you're putting some dates next to your goals to make sure they actually happen. Something that might help you select your goals and make them stick is the acronym of S.M.A.R.T. goals.

S.M.A.R.T. GOALS

S.M.A.R.T. goals are used to help you set goals that you are much more likely to stick to! S.M.A.R.T. is an acronym for Specific, Measurable, Achievable, Relevant, and Timely.

SPECIFIC – Be clear with the goal. Include expectations and avoid generalities.
Example: Buy a 4-bedroom house in Corio by December of this year.

MEASURABLE – Make sure you can track the progress of the goal. Include things like timelines, costs, quantity, and quality.

Example: Pay off my mortgage in 15 years – track this progress by looking at my bank account.

(I'll run you through the process of setting a budget around this in the next chapter).

ATTAINABLE – Make sure you can actually achieve your goal. You want it to be actionable so that it is in your control.
Example: Retire comfortably by contributing $25,000 a year in superannuation. Work with a business coach to make sure my business delivers $2,083 a month without having to stress about it.

RELEVANT – Small goals or goals relevant to you MUST be part of the bigger picture or long-term plan.
Example: Go for a run three days/week to achieve the bigger goal of remaining fit and healthy.

TIME-BASED – Put a date to complete the goal. Stay focused. Use it to inspire you. Work towards it.
Example: You might want to buy a caravan to have a holiday in Robe after Christmas so your goal might be to buy a caravan before December so that you have time to set it up before Christmas.

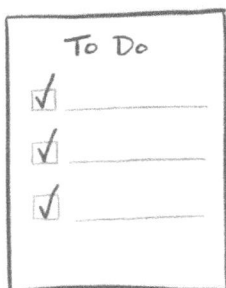

To Do

ACTION ITEM

Set some personal goals

- Have a crack at thinking about some personal goals you want to tackle using the S.M.A.R.T. method.

- Check out the examples list on the following page if you need some help brainstorming some goals.

In the next chapter, I will break down how to set a lot of personal goals that come up, such as how to pay your home loan off quicker, for example.

Examples of Personal Goals

Below is a guide to trigger your own goals. Be sure to add more personal details to them by using the S.M.A.R.T goals – Specific, Measurable, Achievable, Relevance, Timelines – include a date with them!

- Pay off my home.
- Buy/upgrade my home.
- Buy/upgrade my car.
- Take the caravan across Australia.
- Travel to Europe.
- Take the wife and kids to Bali.
- Increase my superannuation.
- Prepare for retirement.
- Build a share portfolio.
- Renovate the house.
- Buy some land to build on later on.
- Build a shed in the backyard.
- Take a 2-week holiday three times a year.
- Take three months off.
- Stop working weekends
- Only work three days/week.
- Have another child.
- Send my kids to private school.

- Have $ amount in savings.
- Save $ amount per week.
- Take time for my hobby one day/week.
- Buy a jet ski.
- Buy a boat (and have time to take it out with my mates regularly).
- Buy a motorbike.
- Buy a caravan
- Buy an investment property.
- Buy more 'toys'.
- Upgrade my personal tools and tech every year.
- Donate $ amount to my favourite charity regularly.
- Do my favourite sport three days/week.
- Take a camping trip.
- Head up north.
- Go skydiving or try something cool.
- Run with the bulls.
- Take a race car for a spin this year.
- Have one full day with the kids, no distractions.
- Take my wife/partner out for dinner every week.
- Cave dive in Mexico.
- Run a marathon.

Chapter Seven

How to Create Big-Ticket Assets

When it comes to personal goal setting, I see a few common themes coming up for tradie owners:

- A lot of you want a goal around paying down your home sooner or buying a home if you don't own one yet.

- Too many of you don't pay yourself superannuation, and you don't have a plan around it.

- The majority of you haven't really thought about setting a plan around the items that will move the needle most on your overall personal wealth position.

Now, don't get me wrong here, setting goals is entirely personal, so you should absolutely focus on the areas that most matter to you. After all, the aim of the game here is to give you your life back and let it be the one of your dreams.

That said, there are four areas where it may be wise to consider setting some personal goals. This does not mean you need to create goals in each area. I just want to get you thinking in terms of Big-Ticket Assets and how you might want to think outside the box in terms of your return on investment.

Ultimately, you don't want to be working until you're dead or your back's well and truly buggered, so it's a good idea to look ahead and see what you might be able to plan for today that will ease the pressure come retirement.

For me, I was forced to start thinking about the reality of this when my personal circumstances changed and I lost 75% of my assets practically overnight. Given I am closer to retirement age than I am away from it, I realized pretty quickly that I'd have to do things differently if I wanted to make sure I was still able to stand on my own two feet when the day came to retire. So, I focus on these Big-Ticket Assets. I don't normally have goals associated with vehicles and boats, as they usually have a lower value (and if they are financed, have a much shorter term), but if lifestyle toys bring you joy and that's where you are in your stage of life, then it's a fantastic goal. Everyone is different so the goals you pick should be unique to you. These are just thinking points for you and may also help to answer a few big questions that come up for my tradie clients.

The Four Big-Ticket Assets

- Property (your home and/or investment property)

- Business Valuation

- Share Portfolio

- Superannuation

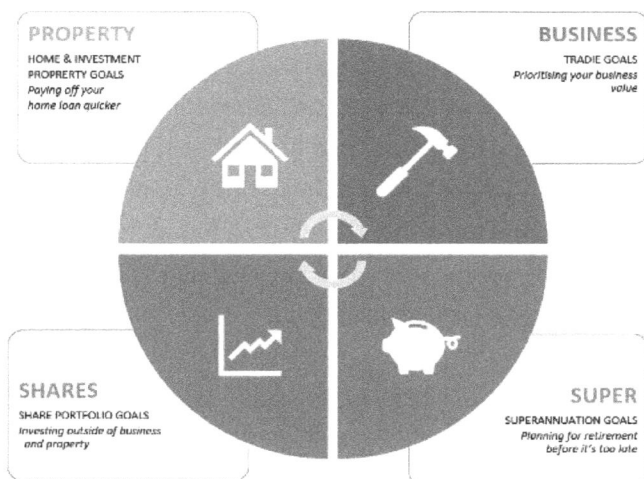

In this section, I am going to walk you through how
to create a financial plan for each of these items
including the "B" word – BUDGET, because the
truth is having a goal around each of these items will
impact your annual spend, which in turn will directly
affect how much money you need your business to
generate for you every year.

Before we get into the meat and potatoes, I just want
to take a moment to say that from my own personal
experience of setting goals and writing them down,
these goals turn into a plan extraordinarily quickly,
and once that happens, they seem to be achieved
even quicker. This is where it gets exciting!

PROPERTY

Having a goal around your home, investment
property, or home loan is a very common goal for
the tradie business owner. But here's the crux: I
rarely meet with anyone that has a system in place
to deliver that goal. I have tested this with all my
clients and many of my friends, and found this to be
true almost all the time. You need a plan in place so
that your property goals happen.

Should I pay off my home loan?

I also need to point out that paying off your home super-fast may not be the smartest thing to do.

It all depends on your age, your views as a couple (if you have a partner), and other opportunities you may have. I always like the concept of the "sleep easy" principle — If you have your house paid off or low loans, and this allows you and your partner to sleep easy, it's worth it. No one wants to be up all night worried about their home loan payments, but everyone has a different appetite to risk. The other option is not to pay off your home faster, but instead, put this money into your business or other investments.

How to Set a Financial Plan Around Your Home Loan

The best thing about setting a loan goal is that it is dead easy. Just find an online loan calculator on your bank's website. I personally use the Commbank home loan repayment calculator but anyone will do.

www.commbank.com.au/digital/home-buying/ calculator/home-loan-repayments

Let's look at a typical example:

Currently you have a home loan of $490K, 25 years, 3% interest. Repayments are $2,323/month.

Suppose you have a goal to pay it off in 15 years.
Using the online loan calculator, simply adjust
the loan term to suit. Using the same example, the
repayments would now be $3,383/month.

So, all you need to do now is put this new payment
on autopilot to make sure it happens. That is, set up
a payment of this new amount to be direct-debited
from your bank account. I'm a fan of setting up
automatic payments directly from your business
account to your home loan account so this money
never actually lands in your savings account and
you're not tempted to spend it!

To recap: the goal is to pay off your house in 15
years, and the plan to make it happen is to set up
automatic payments of $3,383/month.

Easy, right?

Of course, there will be some folks out there who
are worried they're unable to make payments at this
rate. In fact, you might be thinking, "Ah, yeah right,
Hugh! I'll just add an extra $1,000 on the mortgage
each month, no problem." And who knows, maybe
you're being sarcastic in your response! Remember:
our bigger aim here is to make the BUSINESS
provide enough income to achieve this. Start with

the dream, set the goal, and get your business to deliver. We'll go more into how your business will deliver this figure as we dive deeper into the book.

FYI – I have an ambitious goal of paying off my own mortgage in nine years and I ran this same plan, set it on autopilot and simply got busy running my business to take care of the numbers for me. Job done! The debt's getting taken care of in the background and I sleep like a baby knowing I won't be stuck paying off a huge chunk of money twenty years down the road!

Should I pay off my investment property or my home?

In a similar manner to your home, you may want to have a goal to pay off an investment property. You would obviously tackle it in the same manner. I often get asked this question: "Which is more important to pay off, your investment or your house?

My response is usually this: pay off NON-tax-deductible loans like your house or a personal car BEFORE an investment property. That said, this is a great question to ask your accountant.

GOAL SETTING TIP

Use an online loan calculator to experiment with the loan term to work out how many years you would like to pay down your loan if this is a personal goal of yours.

BUSINESS

Hopefully the "How to Value Your Business" chapter highlighted that your business value can increase significantly with higher multiple earnings! So, it's wise to realise that the overall worth of your business affects your overall wealth position. This will be crucial to you if you are ever in a position to sell.

This is why you might want to consider having a goal around your business value. I know a lot of tradie owners have a goal around business profits, which is also a great idea.

We'll talk about this more in the business section, but taking a moment to think about how you might be able to increase the overall value may also be a good starting point.

Obviously, it's important to realise that business inherently comes with more risk, which as a business owner, you accept with the expectation of higher returns. However, it is a mistake to think that it isn't worth investing in anything else.

For example, if you have a major Occupational Health and Safety (OH&S) incident, or a large job with a major commercial problem like a major builder going into receivership, your business value could quickly become nothing.

Again, while everyone has a different acceptance of risk, I do recommend investing outside of your business such as with your home, in shares and/or with an investment property — as a diversification strategy to protect yourself and your family.

So, when it comes to business value, think whether or not setting a goal around this is important to you. If so, come up with a dollar amount on how much you want to see it increase and when you want to see it happen, so we know what we need to do in your business to deliver that growth.

GOAL SETTING TIP

Work with a business coach to help you not only hit this target, but also find out if your goal is reasonable when taking into account your bigger personal dreams.

SHARES

Having a share portfolio is usually not the first investment that comes to mind for tradies!

I get it. You work in the construction scene and you understand how all the trades work together so you're much more interested in investing in property.

While I am no financial planner, I have been investing in shares since I was a teenager, and while I've certainly made mistakes along the way (got a bit too cocky for my own good), I have definitely seen the upside of investing in them.

One little known advantage of shares is that it is possible to sell some of your portfolio. For example, if you wanted to renovate your kitchen you could simply sell a portion of your shares. You're definitely not able to sell 10% of your house to do the same thing!

Shares vs Property
Which One Is Better?

Shares vs property is a hotly debated topic and leads to a lot of debate when trying to determine which one is best.

Here's the answer for you. It is highly dependent on what the actual assets are! Is it a "good" property or "bad" property? Is it a "good" company or a "bad" one? Is the asset giving you a decent return or not?

Whatever your preference, returns are relatively similar and investing in both provide diversity. That said, if I could only afford one investment property or a bunch of shares, I would personally choose the shares based on the following example that happened to my brother.

My brother lives in Darwin and has two investment properties. These are both based in Darwin and were purchased between 2005 and 2008. At the time he bought them, the market was going up strongly, but in 2014 at the end of several government and infrastructure projects, the market dropped 30%. Even now, in 2022, it's not back to the 2014 prices.

While the above scenario isn't necessarily true for every property and certainly not in every location, it has made me think twice about investing in property, particularly if you don't have genuine expert help or are just buying because the market is hot.

The same is true for shares. If you are not skilled in selecting, purchasing, and managing shares, you will need to do some learning and possibly look at getting some expert help if need be. Share brokers are your "go-to" for advice and also provide the platform to purchase shares. You can also purchase shares without advice through online trading platforms. Most major banks have their own trading platform. I personally use Commonwealth Securities (Commsec), but look for yourself and see what's out there.

One of my clients recently wanted to start a portfolio, so he rushed out and read three books on the topic and bought a few shares on an online platform valued at about $10,000.

While your risk appetite might be different, this particular client is intending to muck around with this level of investment to improve his skills and knowledge.

He is happy with the level of risk vs reward.

Four Basic Principles When Buying Shares

When starting out, there's a lot of learning when it comes to shares. But there are four basic principles that are important to consider:

- Build up to at least five shares to reduce your risk if one isn't performing.

- At first, only buy shares in the ASX Top 50 Index and don't get too excited by very small companies or cheap stocks.

- If you buy them yourself, you will need to manage them as opposed to "buy and forget".

- Always use a stop loss or protect the maximum you can lose on a particular share, i.e., sell if a share loses more than 10% from your purchase price so as to protect your capital.

From my perspective, you need to get more professional help when your portfolio starts to grow in size. Think about it like this: If you were to buy a secondhand excavator for $70,000, you would probably get an expert mechanic to check it over to make sure it's a good investment. But, if you were buying a $5,000 second-hand ute, you might forgo a full inspection and simply take the risk. The same thinking is true for your share portfolio.

GOAL SETTING TIP

For a share portfolio goal, I just put a set amount toward the trading bank account that could be invested if the timing was right.

SUPERANNUATION

Superannuation is complex to understand at the best of times, but as a business owner, there's another level to add to the mix.

Let's start with the purpose.

The purpose behind superannuation in the government's eyes is so that you can afford to live without the need for government assistance in retirement.
For employees, this is quite simple in that we employers contribute to super for them. But for business owners, if we don't pay ourselves a wage, then we are not forced to contribute to superannuation. We are presumed to build up a superannuation portfolio under our own direction or have investments outside of super.

This is where most business owners I meet with have their blinkers on. They simply do not have a plan for their income in retirement! Very few tradie owners have much super at all and they're not focused on building assets.

I get that trying to work out how much income you will need in 15 years' time is difficult for anyone to predict. But here's the reality: There's no excuse for not having a basic plan in place. If you want an excellent plan, this is where financial planners and accountants can help, but at the bare minimum, you need a basic plan.

Unless your idea of fun is working you're arse off just to retire broke, then you need a plan for super in place. The pension won't be enough for you. Plain and simple.

For my current clients, I focus on the facts, develop a basic plan, and then refer to experts when the time is right.

So, hitting some of the biggest questions:

Should you be paying yourself super?

I recommend that superannuation and investments are part of your strategy. And, yes, this also means investing in your business.

Obviously with superannuation, it's locked away until retirement age whereas with an investment, it can be sold and used if needed, so a more accurate answer is:

You should be putting money away for retirement — this could be a mix of super and investments.

How much better off will you be if you pay super?

Most business owners use an accountant to submit their end-of-financial-year annual tax return and as a business owner, money that you put into super will have 15% tax attributed to up the value of $27,500.

If you happen to pay the same amount to yourself, you will have to pay tax at your personal tax rate. Let's say that even at a modest taxable income between $45K and $120K, this would fall into the 32.5% taxation bracket, so you would be 17.5% better off by putting it into super. At the 37% tax bracket, you would be even better off.

How much do you need in retirement?

Every year, The ASFA (Association of Super Funds of Australia) publishes how much the average person needs to live in retirement. At the time of writing this (2022), the answer is about $70,000/year for couples to live comfortably if they own their own home.

Most people I speak to however, believe they will need more than that, especially if they've become accustomed to a certain way of living (this is another story).

HUGH BOWMAN

To add more uncertainty to the mix is knowing how much $70K in 2022 will be by the time you retire. Let's say you retire in 15 years. The answer is about $103K based on a conservative CPI rate. These calculations are a bit too tricky for this book, but I can personally run them through for you if you're interested.

What size does your super portfolio need to be to retire?

Again, this is tricky to work out as it depends on when you retire. At the moment, you will need a portfolio size of $1.4 – $2.0M. Now don't be despondent at such a large super portfolio required. If you are young, you have plenty of time to sort it out.

If you are nearing retirement, it's much more difficult, but there are other options for you such as continuing to work part time or moving into a different occupation that pays more. You might also end up inheriting something, although to me this sounds quite risky to rely on.

It's probably safe to say the regulation of super has a history of change with different governments and probably will continue to.Another handy tip to know as a business owner: If you sell your business, up to $1.6M can be transferred directly into super.

Below you'll see an example of how much super you should currently have based on your age. As you can see, if you are not making voluntary contributions there is a gap at all age levels.

How much Super Should You Have?

Gender	Age	Average Balance	Balance required today for comfortable retirement	Gap
Male	30	$25,520	$61,000	-$35,480
	40	$56,792	$154,000	-$97,208
	50	$111,115	$271,000	-$159,885
	60	$180,944	$430,000	-$249,056
Female	30	$21,765	$61,000	-$39,235
	40	$46,075	$154,000	-$107,925
	50	$87,634	$271,000	-$183,366
	60	$154,896	$430,000	-$275,104

How much superannuation you should have based on your age. Source: Canstar

So here are the two things that are very important to know:

- There will be lots of change with super in the future.
- It's vitally important that you have a basic plan for retirement.

If you want further help navigating this area, I can help or you can chat with a qualified financial planner or accountant.

To give you an idea how passionate I am about this, when I found this all out myself and realized how big my own gap was, I immediately pivoted to making sure my business provided an extra $25,000 to pay into my super each year.

This is obviously a significant increase. The amount you choose will be dependent on your own situation, goals and age, but I strongly suggest putting some thought into this area, especially if you don't currently pay yourself any super at all.

GOAL SETTING TIP

If you know you don't have enough super now and you can afford to put as much as possible into it, it's a good idea to consider putting in $25K/year. Of course, there is no limit to how much you contribute, just be mindful it will incur a higher level of tax.

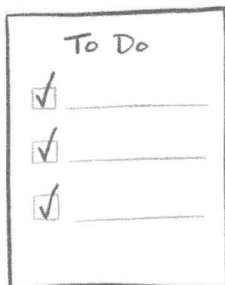

To Do

☑ _____
☑ _____
☑ _____

ACTION ITEM

Set Some Big-Ticket Asset Goals

- Work out what's important to you in each big-ticket area - property (your home and/ or investments), business value, shares and super.

- Write down your goal/s in each area (if you have one), making sure you use the S.M.A.R.T method (Specific, Measurable, Attainable, Relevance and Time-based).

- Put a dollar figure on how much you will need to achieve each goal and take action on them as soon as you can.

Examples of Big-Ticket Asset Goals

This is a guide only. You need to add more personal details to them.

Remember to turn your own goals into S.M.A.R.T goals – Specific, Measurable, Achievable, Relevance, Timelines – include a date with them!

- Pay off my home loan of $500,000 in 15 years.

- Buy a home worth $750,000 this year.

- Buy an investment property worth $900,000 next year.

- Grow my business value by $200,000 in the next two years.

- Aim to increase my business multiple by one over the next 12 months.

- Double my business value in the next three years.

- Start a share portfolio with $10,000.

- Invest $500 in shares each month.

- Pay myself an extra $20,000 in super each year.

- Pay myself an extra $200/week into my super account.

Chapter Eight

Making The Budget Cool Again

Let's clear the elephant in the room. Everyone hates the word "budget." Just utter the word and it makes most people cringe. It might even make you feel sick, or restricted, or broke, or suddenly like you need to stop having a life!

But here's the flipside of having a budget in place that works FOR you and doesn't give you all of the frustration: You suddenly feel in control, at peace, and totally ahead of the game!

So how great would it be if I told you that setting a personal budget is not only worthwhile, but it's also practically painless for a business owner?

Here's the secret: When you're a business owner, you get to ditch all the effort and annoyance of sticking to a budget. All you need to do is work out how much you need each year and then you get your business to deliver that amount! Pretty pain-free if you ask me.

So, what we're about to do in this chapter is not really budgeting as you'd commonly think about it. We're going to work out exactly how much money you need each year. We'll do this by working out how much you currently spend, add in the costs of your new goals, and come up with the dollar amount you need your business to deliver for you each year. Simple!

I call this my "Big-Ticket Budget". You put the big things in place so you don't get stuck on the little pesky stuff. You can further tweak that if you want, but I reckon you've probably got other stuff to do!

You simply need to know what figure you're working towards for your business so you can live your dream life! If you want to knock this out of the park and take your money management to the next level (and there's absolute merit in that), go check out some nitty-gritty budgets or money systems out there.

Ultimately, there are many options on how to put a budget together, but I reckon it has to come down to something you can work with.

So, "idiot-proofing" and just getting it done is exactly what we're doing here! This method works for many business owners that I know, and I personally run it myself. It's not going to take over your life. It's an easy, tradie-friendly, time-tested "budget" that consists of three simple steps.

The Big-Ticket Budget

Here's a quick snapshot of my simple big-ticket budget (BTB):

Step 1: Work out your base living costs.

Step 2: Add in the costs to achieve your big-ticket goals.

Step 3: Add in the costs to achieve your other yearly goals.

Let's quickly run through each step before I take you through a "real life" example. You'll see it in action for a client and you can get the details for my free BTB tool if you want the process to be even easier.

Step 1: Work out your base living costs

Base living costs include all the costs to run your house except the mortgage. This includes stuff like food, utilities, school fees, clothing and rent. These are the bare essentials to satisfy your current needs. The quickest way to work this out is to look at your bank statement and see how much you're spending on all this.

When this happens, some people choose to dive deep on the particulars to increase savings or reduce wastage. Sometimes the act of actually seeing how much you're spending motivates you to cut back. I prefer to focus my attention elsewhere. I just want to know that what I need will be covered.

A simple way to manage your base living costs is to work out how much the total cost is per week and set up an automatic transfer that dumps this amount into your everyday account on the same day each week. Once this money is in your account, go ahead and spend it on base living cost items.

It's pretty easy to see if your bank account balance is increasing or decreasing over time so you will know if you're paying yourself the right amount.

Step 2: Add in the costs to achieve your big-ticket goals

Halleluiah! The process just got even simpler! You just completed this step in the previous chapter. Well done.

FYI – I find that totaling the costs of each goal to come up with both a yearly and monthly total is really helpful.

For example, if your goal is to pay off your $490,000 mortgage in 15 years and you know this means you need to spend $3,383/month to achieve it, you'd multiply this number by 12 so you can see your yearly commitment as well. (In this example it would be $40,600).

Do this for each of your big-ticket asset.

Step 3: Add in the costs to achieve your other yearly goals

Next, look at the things you want to do this year - some of the personal goals you've thought about. Again, these usually come from your W.I.S.H List (What I Should Have). They are the dreams you are prioritizing and, as such, are turning into goals to complete this year.

For example: You've decided you want to tick off that 2-week holiday to your dream location in November this year. You've checked out the flight costs and have a rough idea on how much you'll need for accommodations, meals and spending money. All together it will cost you about $8,000, so you'd simply add this amount into your yearly budget as well as your other goals.

FREE TOOL: Big-Ticket Budget

If you would like a FREE tool to help with the above exercise, visit **www.wealthytradie.com.au/freestuff.** It includes sections to list your goals, big-ticket assets, etc., so you can monitor what you've allocated to what. See the following example that demonstrates how this budget works in real life.

The Big-Ticket Budget in Action - Meet Brendon and Sue

Brendon is an electrical contractor. His business works primarily with first-home builds, though sometimes he and his team do some small maintenance projects here and there. When Brendon (48) and his wife Sue (43) came to see me, I found out that Brendon worked really long hours, Sue worked in the business too, primarily doing the admin stuff, yet neither of them earnt a wage from the business.

They paid themselves a draw when they needed it, and that was pretty much it. But here's the thing: both of them were absolutely exhausted and worse yet, they weren't sure if they were even making enough money for all the effort! It was clear their business was running THEM. They had lost sight of why they went into business in the first place.

When I asked Brendon and Sue to explain their personal goals and what they really wanted in life, Brendon said, "Nah mate, nothing personal… just business!"

Well unlike you and I, he hadn't yet realized that getting clear on your personal dreams and goals is the key to unlocking real (and sustainable) business success! Instead, he was stuck working all the time with not much money to show for it, and with no real reason as to why he and his wife were busy busting their guts.

They were missing out on spending quality time with friends and family, and pretty much dedicating their entire lives to being stressed out and responsible for everything!

Brendan was challenged by this idea at first, whereas Sue could see the link pretty quickly. Once he saw it, boy was it worth it!

When we got going into the personal stuff, which again is a vital step, I found out they had a couple of teenage kids — Kate (16) and Michael (18). They live in Belmont and along with having $490,000 outstanding on their home loan, they also bought an investment property two years ago in Yackandandah just before Covid-19 hit.

Instead of paying down their home loan quicker, they opted to take the equity out of their family home and put it towards this purchase. This is a great example where you might not decide to have a goal for your home loan because you are investing your hard-earned money somewhere else.

Among many things, they were questioning if buying an investment property was actually the right decision. With everything going on with Covid, they hadn't been able to get anyone to rent it.

Curious, I ran their numbers on The Wealth Tracker and realized this property had gone up from $450,000 to $600,000 since the time they had bought it! So even though the property wasn't rented, it was clear to see that the capital growth gain was magnificent. A $150,000 increase is certainly not a bad outcome in a couple of years! Obviously, you need to consider the cost to cover the rent (which is significantly less in this case), but given they'd definitely be able to get someone in to rent it soon, from my point of view, it was a beauty!

This really highlights the importance of measuring your overall net wealth position before making your decisions. Even though this is just an "on-paper" increase, it helps show how much something is likely to be worth – and, yes, it will capture whether the property is a dud if it's continually going down in value.

After filling the rest of their personal finances into The Wealth Tracker and honing in on their personal goals, both for their big-ticket assets and other things they wanted to achieve and do within the year, we moved on to Brendon and Sue's big-ticket budget.

Here's what it looked like:

BIG TICKET BUDGET			
	Calendar year	Monthly amount	Notes/Goals
Year	20XX		
BASE LIVING COSTS	64560	5380	
BIG TICKET ASSETS			
Home -	40600	3383	Goal to pay off in 15 years
Super	20000	1667	Contribute $20k/year minimum
Shares	20000	1667	3 year goal - share Portfolio $60k
Investment property	18000	1500	Balance after rental income to pay off in 15 years
YEARLY GOALS			
Family holidays	8000	667	Family to Tasmania
Personal holidays	7000	583	Cape York motorbike trip
Holiday house	0		Est $650k - Need deposit of $190k
Workshop for Business	0		Est $500k for 150m2
Caravan	0		Est $80,000
Ski boat	10000	833	Est $70k - Put $10k away per year
Total - Required	188160	15680	

Let's break it down.

Brendon and Sue had a rough idea of how much they were spending on the basics. To double- check, they opened up their bank app on their phone and, yes, they could see that their transactions for food, clothing, utilities and school fees totaled $5,380 for the month.

This meant they would transfer themselves $1,242 each week to cover the cost of their basic living expenses. As you can see, we have put this total in our free big-ticket budget tool.

Next, we move on to the big-ticket assets. That is, our goals around the "Big 4" assets if we have them: property, super, shares. Please note: we don't need to include any goals around our business value here as we are dealing purely with our personal needs and wants.

As mentioned, their family home loan was sitting at $490,000. Because they had already purchased their investment property, they decided they wanted to put some goals around chipping away at their mortgage and putting extra cash towards the investment property loan as well.

Just like our first example, they decided their goal was to pay off their home loan in 15 years. We banged this information into an online loan calculator and worked out that their monthly commitment to achieve this goal was $3,383. Likewise, they also had a goal to pay off the remaining balance on their investment property in 15 years.

We worked out that they would prioritize getting someone in there to rent it ASAP (which they were now confident could happen) and calculated that they would need to spend $1,500 each month of their own money to pay down the loan in fifteen years.

So, we put those numbers into our big-ticket budget. (As you can see, we include a yearly amount, too).

And because they really understood the importance of diversification (spreading your risk by investing in other things outside of the business), Brendon and Sue decided to set themselves an ambitious goal of investing $20,000 in shares throughout the course of the year. This equates to $1,667 a month, so we'll need to make sure this amount is also factored in when we determine how much the business will need to deliver each year.

Next up, is superannuation. Boy, had they overlooked this one! Because they didn't pay either of themselves a wage, they weren't forced to pay themselves super which meant that Brendon and Sue RARELY paid themselves a voluntary contribution at all. The result? They did not have nearly enough super in their account and they weren't spring chickens! At 48 and 43, Brendon and Sue really needed to consider having a plan in place for retirement.

While the investment property and the share portfolio would help with the amount of money they would have access to when they finally hung up the boots, they absolutely needed to pump money into their super account so they wouldn't go hungry come retirement! They quickly agreed to a goal of $20,000 a year as a good place to start.

As we entered this amount into the big-ticket budget, we could see the numbers starting to add up. They needed way more than they thought and we weren't done! They still had their personal goals for the year to go.

We needed to set some cash aside for holidays. Their kids, Kate and Michael, were growing up and it was only a matter of time before they didn't want to hang out with their parents anymore. They were already pushing it, but they thought a 2-week holiday to the Gold Coast after not being able to travel for so long would tie them over. So, we factored in $8,000 for this family holiday as well as an extra $7,000 for a Cape York motorbike trip.

The most exciting of all, Brendon really wanted a ski boat. He'd been eyeing one for years, but he never thought he could afford it. But because we had discussed the importance of dreams coming true, he thought, "You know what? Let's make it happen." He reckoned the age of 55 was a nice time to own a boat. And it would give him enough time to set aside some money for it.

We estimated the boat would be around $70,000, which would mean they would need to set aside $10,000 each year if he wanted it for his 55th birthday. So, into our big-ticket budget it goes.

Now that we've got all the costs in (both cost per month and cost per year), the big-ticket budget tool automatically spits the total amount needed each year. In this case, Brendon and Sue need $188,160 this year to cover it all.

At first they thought, "No way. That's way more than we're drawing out of the business right now!" Later on in our conversation, we discovered that they didn't actually know how much they were drawing out of their business because they just transferred any ol' lump sum when they needed it.

The truth was yes, it WAS more than they were paying themselves. It covered everything from making sure their dreams happen and, the biggest one for Brendon and Sue, ensuring they have enough for retirement.

But there was absolutely no need to panic. Remember the secret? The business is funding this cost. And now that we had our yearly number, we knew EXACTLY what we were aiming for and what levers we'd need to pull to make sure the business delivered it.

We'll come back to Brendon and Sue and what we focus on in their business to make sure it pays them at least $188,160 each year, but for now, go ahead and create your own Big Ticket Budget.

You're welcome to use my free tool available at:
 www.wealthytradie.com.au/freestuff
or any other budgeting app you find useful.

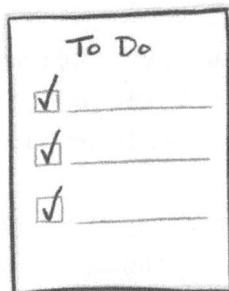

ACTION ITEM

Create your own big-ticket budget

- Work out how much your base living costs are.

- Add in the costs to achieve your big-ticket assets (you should have this information already from the last chapter).

- Add in the costs to achieve your other yearly goals.

If you want to speed up the process and get your yearly number generated for you, please use my FREE big-ticket budget tool available at **www.wealthytradie.com.au/freestuff.**

Your Next Steps

Congratulations on getting this far and hopefully knocking off at least some of the hardest work you can do…. working on yourself! Having created your big-ticket budget is light years ahead of the average business owner. The next big steps are how to turn your business into your wealth generator and make your business work for you.

This is exactly how we help business owners through the coaching practice. We help them identify:

- The proven strategies and "business hacks" to get their time back.

- How to control cashflow and navigate the finance stuff so their business funds their personal wealth both today and in retirement.

- What action to take (and prioritize) in their trades business starting now.

Imagine if your business paid for your dream lifestyle, literally all of it. Not just for today, but even when you put down the tools for good and retire.

Imagine NOT being flat out or on the go all the time, and instead being level-headed, clear and respected because you know you've got all of the time, money and resources behind you to take confident action in your business that benefits everyone.

And finally, imagine customers literally knocking on your door and leaving rave reviews about what it was like to work with your company, celebrating with a team who loves working for you, and coming home to a family who feels taken care of and grateful to have you in their life.
How good would that feel?

See, the thing is, this is entirely possible for you and every tradie owner out there. We've just been fed a lie that we need to bust our guts to get work, keep work, and earn a decent living, but this is a myth. Working around the clock leads to exhaustion and frustration, not real wealth. And real wealth is not just about the dollars. Sure, money absolutely plays a role, but real wealth is also about having time, energy, optimal health and great relationships.

Be honest: As it currently stands, is your business currently generating REAL wealth for you? If not, we need to make some changes beginning right now.

Let's get one thing clear: Performing a trade and owning a business is not the same thing! As the owner you are exactly that - the owner, not the operator. So, you need to park the hands-on trades stuff for a moment and focus on business because here's the trick - your business is your key to real wealth.

Unlike an employee who MUST hand over their time and effort in order to get paid, a business owner is in a magnificent position where we don't have to do this if we know how to run our business correctly and effectively. We pay someone else to do the labor, which gives us our time and energy back, and provided we're earning a profit in the process which we should ALWAYS be, we get paid for someone doing the hard work for us.

Best of all, when we play our cards right, we can purposely design the business to spit out enough cash for us to live our dream lifestyle. And because nobody's dream lifestyle involves being sick, broke, exhausted, criticized or lonely, this means you'll be on the home run to real wealth! Very nice indeed.

So, what do we need to do in your business to turn it into your wealth generator instead of your pain in the arse? If you want help with that right now, let's start a conversation.

Work With Me

If you're sick of working all the time and aren't sure where all the money is for all your hard work, or if you know there's a gap in your skills and you need help building wealth through your trades business, I can help in one of three ways:

1. Private One-On-One Coaching

Here we sit down together and work one-on-one to build your business and get it generating the wealth you're after. Because every business (and indeed every business owner) is different, this is tailored business coaching to suit your unique needs, goals and aspirations. As a licensed ActionCOACH Business Coach, I am experienced in, and able to assist you with, the strategic design and implementation of activities such as time management, systems, recruitment, teambuilding, financial reporting, sales and marketing, owner motivation and more.

The first step in this process is a free strategy session where I get to know you and your business and walk you through the coaching process to determine how I can best serve you and your business during our one-on-one time together. I like to get my clients results so my coaching process comes with a guarantee.
I meet all my clients face-to-face to make sure we're on the same page when it comes to maximizing the performance of their business.

I have an office in Geelong where you can literally walk in and have a chat with me and I only work with tradies, so I understand your business unlike some other coaches who sit in suits all day! I've been in the business for over a decade and I'm ready and willing to get you results.

If you're keen to build your wealth and get tangible results in your business starting today, please head to www.actioncoachgeelong.com.au or call me directly on 0409 402 474 for a free no-obligation coaching session.

2. The Wealthy Tradie Workshop

This is full-day live event where I walk you through The Wealthy Tradie system in its entirety and we cover all the critical activities to build wealth through your business together. You will have the opportunity to ask me any questions you have and will walk away with a personalized business and wealth plan that you can put into place immediately. This workshop is unique to tradie business owners and will give you the mindset to uncover your personal dreams and goals, as well as the proven process to get your business delivering them!

The aim of the workshop is to tie all of these together and make sure you retire wealthy and happy, while having a great time along the way.

HUGH BOWMAN

This is a live event that I run only at specific times throughout the year, so spaces are limited and you must get in quick to secure your spot. If you are a current client of mine, this event is completely free to you. If you would like to find out more about this live workshop please visit:

www.wealthytradie.com.au/workshop
or call me directly on **Ph: 0409 402 474.**

3. Group Coaching

This is suited to tradie owners who are just starting out or who are running a one-man business. While you're still spending a serious chunk of your time on the tools, you see a huge opportunity to grow and improve the way you operate. For this reason, you've recognized the need for a coach, but for cashflow and time reasons, you're happy to learn the business fundamentals alongside two or three other business owners in a similar position.

You will need to be a self-starter and recognize that the work we achieve together in a group setting will never be as tailored as one-on-one coaching; however, you will absolutely get benefit from this level of coaching as well as the unique opportunity to learn from other tradie owners in a similar position as you. If you're keen to find out more about group coaching, please visit:

www.actioncoachgeelong.com.au

.

If you're finding yourself working all the time, or are stressed and overwhelmed in your trades business, it's time to pivot to the easier and smarter way of doing things. Invest in yourself and start seeing results today. This is a proven system to follow and you don't need to go it alone or struggle when you simply don't have to, mate!

I want to encourage you to contact me or my team. There is a better way to do business and I know I can help.

Let's get you building wealth through your trades business!

To your success,

Hugh Bowman
hugh@actioncoachgeelong.com.au
www.actioncoachgeelong.com.au
Ph: 0409 402 474